CONTENTS

What can astrology do for me? 2

What is astrology? 4

Your Sun sign 10

Your Rising sign 20

Your Moon sign 28

Elements 38

We are family 44

Best of friends 54

Your birthday log 64

Lucky in love 78

Life at school 86

WHAT CAN ASTROLOGY
do for me?

Astrology is a powerful tool for self-awareness. The idea that we are all connected – that the shifting energies of the Sun, Moon and planets above affect us here on Earth – is an ancient and philosophical belief. Astrology isn't fortune-telling – it can't predict your future and it doesn't deal in absolutes. It simply says that you are part of the universe around you, and by studying the stars, it's possible to learn more about yourself.

Why is this so important? Because the better understanding you have of your own inner make-up – your skills, your talents, your needs and your fears – the more insight you gain into why you act the way you do. And this gives you choices, empowering you to make changes and to build on your strengths. It makes it easier to feel confident and to accept yourself, quirks and all.

There are countless daily horoscopes in newspapers, magazines and online. But this book looks at more than just your star sign, which is only a small part of your personality picture. It helps you to find your Rising sign, which was appearing over the Eastern horizon at the time of your birth, and has a lot to tell you about the way others see you. You can also work out your Moon sign, which reveals the real you deep down inside, giving you the chance to get to grips with your innermost emotions, desires, fears and obsessions.

With a clearer picture of who you are, life becomes less complicated. Instead of trying to live up to others' expectations and being someone you're not, you can work instead on becoming the best version of yourself possible – someone who understands their talents and needs, who is perfectly unique and is happy.

What is ASTROLOGY?

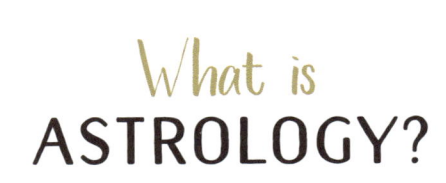

The stars and planets have always inspired a sense of wonder. The ancient peoples of Babylonia, Persia, Egypt, Greece and India were all fascinated by the cycles of the Moon, the rising and setting of the Sun, the position of the constellations, and what it all meant. As these civilizations developed, they connected what they saw in the sky with the people and events on Earth, and astrology was born.

In ancient times, astrology was used to help monarchs rule. Kings and emperors would employ astrologers to predict the weather, speak to the gods and help manage the country.

Modern astrology has evolved to help ordinary people like you and me understand ourselves better – how we behave, how we feel about each other and how we can make the best of who we are.

THE SIGNS OF THE ZODIAC

Today we know that the planets revolve around the Sun, but astrology is based on how we see the solar system from here on Earth. The Zodiac is a group of 12 constellations that, from our viewpoint, seem to rotate around Earth over the course of a year, like a huge wheel. These constellations are named after the animals and objects that our ancestors thought they looked most like – the ram, the lion, the scorpion and so on. Your Sun sign tells you which of the constellations the Sun was moving through on the day you were born. The signs have a natural order that never varies, beginning with Aries. The dates given on the right change slightly from year to year for the same reasons we have a leap year – each of our days is slightly longer than 24 hours. If you were born at the beginning or end of a sign, called 'the cusp', it's worth checking your Sun sign online to be sure.

ARIES March 21–April 20	**LIBRA** September 23–October 22
TAURUS April 21–May 21	**SCORPIO** October 23–November 21
GEMINI May 22–June 21	**SAGITTARIUS** November 22–December 21
CANCER June 22–July 22	**CAPRICORN** December 22–January 20
LEO July 23–August 23	**AQUARIUS** January 21–February 19
VIRGO August 24–September 22	**PISCES** February 20–March 20

THE FOUR ELEMENTS

*Each Sun sign is associated with one of four elements –
Fire, Earth, Air and Water.*

FIRE

Aries, Leo, Sagittarius
Fire signs are passionate, dynamic and temperamental.
They mix well with: Fire and Air types

EARTH

Taurus, Virgo, Capricorn
Earth signs are practical, cautious and reliable.
They mix well with: Water and Earth types

AIR

Gemini, Libra, Aquarius
Air signs are quick, curious and adventurous.
They mix well with: Air and Fire types

WATER

Cancer, Scorpio, Pisces
Water signs are sensitive, emotional and kind.
They mix well with: Earth and Water types

THE PLANETS

Astrology looks at the positions of the stars and planets at the time and place of your birth. The Sun and Moon aren't technically planets, but they're referred to that way by astrologers for ease of use. The Sun is a great place to start – it's the most important object in the solar system. Your Sun sign describes the essence of your identity, and says a great deal about your potential – the person you might become.

The position the Moon held in the sky at the time of your birth has a strong influence, too. It describes your emotions – how you feel deep inside. It can give you a better understanding of what you need to feel loved and cared for.

And there's also your Rising sign. This is the sign of the Zodiac that was appearing over the Eastern horizon at the time of your birth. It tells you more about how you interact with the world around you, especially to new situations. It's the filter through which you perceive the world and the impression you give to others on first meeting. Which means it's also how others often see you.

The positions of the other planets – Venus, Mercury, Mars, etc – in your birth chart all have their own effect. But these three taken together – Sun, Moon and Rising sign – will give you a deeper understanding of who you are and what you could become, your strengths and weaknesses, your real self.

Your SUN sign

VIRGO

August 24–September 22

SYMBOL
The Maiden

ELEMENT
Earth

RULING PLANET
Mercury

BIRTHSTONE
Sapphire

COLOUR
Beige

BODY PART
Digestive system

DAY OF THE WEEK
Wednesday

FLOWER
Buttercup

CHARACTER TRAITS
Dedicated, orderly, humble

KEY PHRASE
'I analyse'

YOUR SUN SIGN

When people talk about astrology and ask about your star sign, they're referring to your Sun sign. It tells you which of the 12 constellations of the Zodiac the Sun was moving through on the day you were born. This makes it easy to work out, which is one of the reasons for its popularity. If you'd like to know the Sun sign of a friend or family member, the table on page 7 shows which days the Sun occupies each of the signs over the course of a year.

The Sun is the heart of your chart – it's the essence of who you are and symbolizes the potential of what you can achieve. It's important to remember, though, that it is only a part of the whole picture when it comes to astrology. It's a wonderful starting point, but there are many other layers encasing your core identity, all of which affect the inner you.

ALL ABOUT YOU

Born with the Sun in Virgo, you have the potential to bring order and structure to any idea, and you have a wonderful eye for detail. In some ways you are a classic example of an Earth sign because you have both feet planted firmly on the ground. You are practical, honest and aren't afraid of hard work: in fact, you love it. Though you might keep that a secret from friends who aren't quite as diligent as you! But in reality you are a fascinating mix. Mercury is your ruling planet, which means you're great at communicating your feelings, so misunderstandings between you and your friends don't happen very often. If they do, you are keen to get things sorted quickly.

Your shyness can sometimes come across as aloofness or as if you think yourself better than your classmates, but there are big rewards for those who push through that initial barrier. You like to be useful and helpful, and you have a strong sense of humanity. Everything you do, you do with care and precision.

Virgos might not be as 'in-your-face' as some of the flashier Zodiac signs, but your ability to put your own needs aside when there's a job to be done gives you a quiet inner strength. And while you'd usually rather play it safe than take any huge risks, you love to support and encourage your friends to follow their dreams, however crazy and 'out there' they might seem. You get a genuine buzz from seeing them reach for the stars, and you're concerned about their health and wellbeing. For that reason alone, you're a great and sought-after friend.

Likes

Routines
Helping others
Cleaning
Feeling healthy
Making lists

Dislikes

Asking for help
Making mistakes
Cruelty

HOW TO BRING OUT YOUR BEST

You like to think and rationalize, and you have bundles of nervous energy. Occasionally all that overthinking can lead to unnecessary stress. When you feel yourself starting to get anxious, try some slow, deep breaths and you'll be surprised at how quickly you will feel back in control.

Cruelty in any shape or form upsets you, so be extra careful about what you watch on TV. Perhaps you could channel that sensitivity and volunteer at an animal shelter? Making a positive change does wonders for confidence levels.

Kind and selfless to a fault, you may feel like you were put on this planet to help others. Just be careful not to forget your own needs when you get wrapped up in the dramas of your friends' lives. After all, you need to make sure you're feeling happy before you can do a great job of helping those closest to you.

You can be surprisingly mature for your age and have high expectations of everyone in your life. When you decide on a goal, you have the determination and perseverance to make it happen. And that analytical mind of yours is a whizz at solving problems. Just be ready to accept that not all of your friends will be as grown-up as you are – sometimes it's okay to be silly and goof around.

Strengths

Thoughtful
Modest
Responsible
Organized
Diligent
Helpful
Smart

Weaknesses

Self-critical
Fussy
Anxious

SECRET FEARS

As a natural communicator, your favourite thing is having friends around, whatever time of day or night (which probably drives your parents crazy!).

This deep desire for companionship and connection means that feelings of loneliness can strike you more quickly than others.

Even though you probably pop up in school yearbooks as 'Most Clever', you can be extremely hard on yourself because you are holding yourself up against your own version of perfection. Your inner self-talk can then become self-critical. Next time this happens, try asking yourself if that's the way you'd speak to a close friend.

Most likely to . . .

Cheer on your friends
Fix something
Rescue a neighbour's cat
Multi-task
Host a sleepover
Be a neat-freak
Keep receipts

YOUR RISING SIGN

Your Rising sign, also known as your Ascendant, is the sign that was rising over the Eastern horizon (the place where the Sun rises each day) when you were born. It describes how you see the world and the people around you and how they see you – the first impression that you give and receive, the image you project and the initial reaction you might have to a new situation. A person with Leo Rising, for example, may strike you as warm and engaging, whereas Pisces Rising is more sensitive and possibly shy. Because the Ascendant is determined by the exact time and place you were born, it is the most personal point in your chart. Many astrologers believe this makes it just as important as your Sun sign.

HOW TO FIND YOUR ASCENDANT

This is where it gets a bit tricky. There's a reason that popular astrology only deals with your Sun sign – your Rising sign can be more difficult to work out. But don't be put off. If you know your Sun sign and your time of birth, you can use the table on the right to give you a good idea. To be totally accurate you do need to take into account factors like time zone and daylight savings, and there are plenty of free online calculators that will do just that.

YOUR HOUR OF BIRTH

YOUR SUN SIGN	6:00 AM to 8:00 AM	8:00 AM to 10:00 AM	10:00 AM to 12:00 PM	12:00 PM to 2:00 PM	2:00 PM to 4:00 PM	4:00 PM to 6:00 PM	6:00 PM to 8:00 PM	8:00 PM to 10:00 PM	10:00 PM to 12:00 AM	12:00 AM to 2:00 AM	2:00 AM to 4:00 AM	4:00 AM to 6:00 AM
ARIES ♈	♉	♊	♋	♌	♍	♎	♏	♐	♑	♒	♓	♈
TAURUS ♉	♊	♋	♌	♍	♎	♏	♐	♑	♒	♓	♈	♉
GEMINI ♊	♋	♌	♍	♎	♏	♐	♑	♒	♓	♈	♉	♊
CANCER ♋	♌	♍	♎	♏	♐	♑	♒	♓	♈	♉	♊	♋
LEO ♌	♍	♎	♏	♐	♑	♒	♓	♈	♉	♊	♋	♌
VIRGO ♍	♎	♏	♐	♑	♒	♓	♈	♉	♊	♋	♌	♍
LIBRA ♎	♏	♐	♑	♒	♓	♈	♉	♊	♋	♌	♍	♎
SCORPIO ♏	♐	♑	♒	♓	♈	♉	♊	♋	♌	♍	♎	♏
SAGITTARIUS ♐	♑	♒	♓	♈	♉	♊	♋	♌	♍	♎	♏	♐
CAPRICORN ♑	♒	♓	♈	♉	♊	♋	♌	♍	♎	♏	♐	♑
AQUARIUS ♒	♓	♈	♉	♊	♋	♌	♍	♎	♏	♐	♑	♒
PISCES ♓	♈	♉	♊	♋	♌	♍	♎	♏	♐	♑	♒	♓

VIRGO 23

WHAT YOUR RISING SIGN SAYS ABOUT YOU

Once you have figured out your Ascendant, you are ready to discover more about how you see the world, and how it sees you.

ARIES RISING

This combination brings a charming, playful energy to your sometimes serious demeanour. You act on impulse and always go the extra distance to deliver the best you can. You like to feel in charge, and others see you as capable, if a little arrogant. You're probably the daredevil of your friendship group, signing up for high-adrenaline activities – there's never a dull moment when you're around. However, with your rush to get everything done in super-fast time, you can end up running around in circles, so learning to cool your jets a little will be of benefit.

TAURUS RISING

You're the person your friends want to go shopping with You love stylish clothes and, even better, you have a real ability to sniff out a bargain. Try to remember that material stuff is best balanced with things that make your soul happy, too. Spending time with loved ones and following passions that make your heart sing are truly priceless. Practical and intelligent, financial security is important to you. Thankfully your brilliant work ethic and dogged perseverance mean you're likely to be successful in whatever you choose to do.

GEMINI RISING

Gemini brings a highly sociable side to your personality; a contrast to the sometimes shy Virgo nature. This means you're more comfortable having an in-depth one-on-one chat, but you're also willing to adapt and fit in with others. Your sharp mind and wide knowledge means you have a tendency to become impatient when friends take their time. Learning to commit to one thing when you're curious about so many things is a challenge, but deep down you have the perseverance and determination to be hugely successful.

CANCER RISING

Cancer's watery nature brings with it deep feelings. You interpret the world around you using your senses and emotions, which means you occasionally read things into a situation that simply aren't there. Don't worry – your friends are probably used to the odd over-reaction and can talk you around pretty quickly. Practical, cautious and determined, this is a winning combination when it comes to business – you are capable of accomplishing whatever you set out to do.

LEO RISING

Leo's unwavering self-confidence gives your modesty a bit of a boost. Around your closest friends, you'll happily goof around and likely lose your shyness. However, when it's time to knuckle down (after all, those essays aren't going to write themselves) you mean business and take real pride in doing the best you can. Whichever profession you are drawn to, your slick organizational skills will quickly be noticed by the boss. And your genuine interest in those around you will make you a popular co-worker, too.

VIRGO RISING

Double Virgo means the essence of your inner self matches the way you deal with others. You are extraordinarily helpful and productive to boot. If a friend has decided they want to throw a party, guess whose mobile phone will be blowing up with messages? It's flattering to be in demand, but don't forget to take care of your own business, too. Tidiness and organization are second nature to you, and your parents may not quite believe their eyes when they peek into your room and find everything 'just so'. You're sure to shine in any professions where analysing and fixing problems is a key skill.

LIBRA RISING

The Libran desire to please everyone adds to Virgo's strong drive to help as much as they can. Your intentions are pure and heartfelt; just remember to regularly check in with yourself, too. After all, directing some of that sweet loving inwards will boost your own resources and make you more able to help others. It's a win-win! You're a born diplomat because you're good at 'reading' people, and whichever career you choose after school, your personal, warm approach to situations will stand you in good stead.

SCORPIO RISING

The blend of Scorpio with Virgo means you move from one thing to another; you feel a need to get things done. This can sometimes make you a bit of mystery to your friends, who are always trying to pin you down. They're more than rewarded for their efforts when they do spend time with you, because you're an intuitive and supportive friend. You know what you want in life and are prepared to put in the work to get it. You have a tendency to hide your emotions and come across as cool and calm – letting others know how you really feel will help you really relax.

SAGITTARIUS RISING

Sagittarius is the undisputed explorer of the Zodiac and wonderfully complements Virgo's huge thirst for new knowledge. A future career as a language teacher may beckon as it will help satisfy both your itchy feet and sharp mind. You're also a strong communicator and hard worker. Spending fun times with your friends is a priority for you, although you also value your independence – you need to learn how to walk the fine line between the two. In school, you'll stand out in subjects that call for problem-solving.

CAPRICORN RISING

This is a happy combination. You're comfortable in your own skin and don't need to beat other people to feel good. Your friends trust your quiet wisdom and level-headedness: there are few dramas here. You can be a little sensitive if you feel your intelligence is being questioned – try to take a step back before you over-react. Your strong work ethic and great practical ideas mean you'll be a huge asset to future employers, but it's key to strike a healthy balance between your professional and home life.

AQUARIUS RISING

This sparky pairing gives you a razor-sharp sense of humour and makes for one of the friendliest combinations. When you're in a sociable mood, you'll likely be the centre of attention at parties thanks to your ability to get along with anyone. Highly intelligent and quietly determined, you may be drawn to social causes and areas where you can make a difference, like science or politics. You also have a talent for practical inventions. You can come across as eccentric or unorthodox, but at heart you are more down to earth.

PISCES RISING

As you might expect for a Water sign, Pisces has a 'go-with-the-flow' approach that balances your 'need-to-know everything' characteristic. You are sincere and considerate and are happy to let others bask in the spotlight. You have a gift for tuning into the feelings of others, and you love to be of help in any way you can. Your challenge is to set goals for yourself and decide on the path you want to take through life – to discover what makes you happy.

Your MOON sign

YOUR MOON SIGN

The Moon rules your emotions and your inner moods, telling you what you need to feel safe, comfortable and loved. Knowing your Moon sign should give you a more complete picture of your unique self, helping you to express needs you might be struggling to understand. Suppose your Sun sign is Aries but being first has never been important to you – a Moon in Virgo may be telling you to hang back and fade into the background. Or you might have the Sun in home-loving Cancer but feel an urge to get out there and see the world. Perhaps that's because your Moon is in freedom-loving Sagittarius.

HOW TO FIND YOUR MOON SIGN

Just like your Rising sign, finding your Moon sign is more complicated than finding your Sun sign. That's because the Moon seems to move so quickly, taking just about a month to pass through all of the constellations. Thankfully, the tables on the right and on the next page make finding it a simple process.

First, find your year of birth. Then locate your birth month at the top of the table. Find your date of birth in the column below it, and this will give you your Moon sign. If your date of birth isn't listed, the one before it is your Moon sign.

For example, suppose your date of birth is 4 March, 1995. The date before this is 2 March, for which the Moon sign is Aries. This would mean your Moon sign is Aries.

JAN	FEB	MAR	APR	MAY	JUN	JUL	AUG	SEP	OCT	NOV	DEC
BORN IN THE YEAR 1995											
2 Aqu	1 Pis	2 Ari	1 Tau	1 Gem	2 Leo	2 Vir	3 Sco	1 Sag	2 Aqu	1 Pis	3 Tau
4 Pis	3 Ari	5 Tau	3 Gem	3 Can	5 Vir	4 Lib	5 Sag	3 Cap	5 Pis	3 Ari	5 Gem
7 Ari	5 Tau	7 Gem	6 Can	6 Leo	7 Lib	6 Sco	7 Cap	5 Aqu	7 Ari	5 Tau	8 Can
9 Tau	8 Gem	10 Can	9 Leo	8 Vir	9 Sco	8 Sag	9 Aqu	7 Pis	9 Tau	8 Gem	10 Leo
12 Gem	10 Can	12 Leo	11 Vir	10 Lib	11 Sag	10 Cap	11 Pis	9 Ari	12 Gem	10 Can	13 Vir
14 Can	13 Leo	14 Vir	13 Lib	13 Sco	13 Cap	12 Aqu	13 Ari	12 Tau	14 Can	13 Leo	15 Lib
16 Leo	15 Vir	17 Lib	15 Sco	15 Sag	15 Aqu	14 Pis	15 Tau	14 Gem	17 Leo	15 Vir	17 Sco
19 Vir	17 Lib	19 Sco	17 Sag	17 Cap	17 Pis	17 Ari	18 Gem	17 Can	19 Vir	18 Lib	19 Sag
21 Lib	19 Sco	21 Sag	19 Cap	19 Aqu	19 Ari	19 Tau	20 Can	19 Leo	21 Lib	20 Sco	21 Cap
23 Sco	22 Sag	23 Cap	21 Aqu	21 Pis	22 Tau	22 Gem	23 Leo	22 Vir	23 Sco	22 Sag	23 Aqu
25 Sag	24 Cap	25 Aqu	24 Pis	23 Ari	24 Gem	24 Can	25 Vir	24 Lib	26 Sag	24 Cap	25 Pis
27 Cap	26 Aqu	27 Pis	26 Ari	26 Tau	27 Can	27 Leo	28 Lib	26 Sco	28 Cap	26 Aqu	28 Ari
30 Aqu	28 Pis	30 Ari	28 Tau	28 Gem	29 Leo	29 Vir	30 Sco	28 Sag	30 Aqu	28 Pis	30 Tau
				31 Can		31 Lib		30 Cap		30 Ari	
BORN IN THE YEAR 1996											
1 Gem	3 Leo	1 Leo	2 Lib	2 Sco	2 Cap	2 Aqu	2 Ari	1 Tau	3 Can	2 Leo	2 Vir
4 Can	5 Vir	3 Vir	4 Sco	4 Sag	4 Aqu	4 Pis	4 Tau	3 Gem	5 Leo	4 Vir	4 Lib
6 Leo	8 Lib	6 Lib	7 Sag	6 Cap	6 Pis	6 Ari	7 Gem	6 Can	8 Vir	7 Lib	6 Sco
9 Vir	10 Sco	8 Sco	9 Cap	8 Aqu	9 Ari	8 Tau	9 Can	8 Leo	10 Lib	9 Sco	9 Sag
11 Lib	12 Sag	10 Sag	11 Aqu	10 Pis	11 Tau	11 Gem	12 Leo	11 Vir	13 Sco	11 Sag	11 Cap
14 Sco	14 Cap	13 Cap	13 Pis	12 Ari	13 Gem	13 Can	14 Vir	13 Lib	15 Sag	13 Cap	13 Aqu
16 Sag	16 Aqu	15 Aqu	15 Ari	15 Tau	16 Can	16 Leo	17 Lib	15 Sco	17 Cap	16 Aqu	15 Pis
18 Cap	18 Pis	17 Pis	17 Tau	17 Gem	18 Leo	18 Vir	19 Sco	18 Sag	19 Aqu	18 Pis	17 Ari
20 Aqu	20 Ari	19 Ari	20 Gem	19 Can	21 Vir	21 Lib	21 Sag	20 Cap	21 Pis	20 Ari	19 Tau
22 Pis	23 Tau	21 Tau	22 Can	22 Leo	23 Lib	23 Sco	24 Cap	22 Aqu	23 Ari	22 Tau	22 Gem
24 Ari	25 Gem	23 Gem	25 Leo	25 Vir	26 Sco	25 Sag	26 Aqu	24 Pis	26 Tau	24 Gem	24 Can
26 Tau	27 Can	26 Can	27 Vir	27 Lib	28 Sag	27 Cap	28 Pis	26 Ari	28 Gem	27 Can	26 Leo
29 Gem		28 Leo	30 Lib	29 Sco	30 Cap	29 Aqu	30 Ari	28 Tau	30 Can	29 Leo	29 Vir
31 Can		31 Vir		31 Sag		31 Pis		30 Gem			31 Lib
BORN IN THE YEAR 1997											
3 Sco	1 Sag	1 Sag	1 Aqu	1 Pis	1 Tau	1 Gem	2 Leo	3 Lib	3 Sco	1 Sag	1 Cap
5 Sag	4 Cap	3 Cap	4 Pis	3 Ari	4 Gem	3 Can	4 Vir	6 Sco	5 Sag	4 Cap	3 Aqu
7 Cap	6 Aqu	5 Aqu	6 Ari	5 Tau	6 Can	5 Leo	7 Lib	8 Sag	8 Cap	6 Aqu	5 Pis
9 Aqu	8 Pis	7 Pis	8 Tau	7 Gem	8 Vir	9 Sco	10 Cap	10 Aqu	12 Pis	8 Pis	8 Ari
11 Pis	10 Ari	9 Ari	10 Gem	9 Can	11 Vir	10 Lib	12 Sag	12 Pis	12 Pis	10 Ari	10 Tau
13 Ari	12 Tau	11 Tau	12 Can	12 Leo	13 Lib	13 Sco	14 Cap	15 Pis	14 Ari	12 Tau	12 Gem
15 Tau	14 Gem	13 Gem	14 Leo	14 Vir	16 Sco	15 Sag	16 Aqu	17 Ari	16 Tau	14 Gem	14 Can
18 Gem	16 Can	16 Can	17 Vir	17 Lib	18 Sag	18 Cap	18 Pis	19 Tau	18 Gem	17 Can	16 Leo
20 Can	19 Leo	18 Leo	19 Lib	19 Sco	20 Cap	20 Aqu	20 Ari	21 Gem	20 Can	19 Leo	19 Vir
23 Leo	21 Vir	21 Vir	22 Sco	22 Sag	22 Aqu	22 Pis	22 Tau	23 Can	23 Leo	21 Vir	21 Lib
25 Vir	24 Lib	23 Lib	24 Sag	24 Cap	24 Pis	24 Ari	24 Gem	25 Leo	25 Vir	24 Lib	24 Sco
28 Lib	26 Sco	26 Sco	27 Cap	26 Aqu	26 Ari	26 Tau	27 Can	28 Vir	28 Lib	26 Sco	26 Sag
30 Sco		28 Sag	29 Aqu	28 Pis	29 Tau	29 Leo	29 Leo	30 Lib	30 Sco	29 Sag	28 Cap
		30 Cap		30 Ari			31 Vir				31 Aqu
BORN IN THE YEAR 1998											
2 Pis	2 Tau	2 Tau	2 Can	2 Leo	3 Lib	3 Sco	2 Sag	3 Aqu	2 Pis	1 Ari	2 Gem
4 Ari	4 Gem	4 Gem	4 Leo	4 Vir	5 Sco	5 Sag	4 Cap	5 Pis	4 Ari	3 Tau	4 Can
6 Tau	7 Can	6 Can	7 Vir	7 Lib	8 Sag	8 Cap	6 Aqu	7 Ari	6 Tau	5 Gem	6 Leo
8 Gem	9 Leo	8 Leo	9 Lib	9 Sco	10 Cap	10 Aqu	8 Pis	9 Tau	8 Gem	7 Can	9 Vir
10 Can	11 Vir	11 Vir	12 Sco	12 Sag	13 Aqu	12 Pis	11 Ari	11 Gem	10 Can	10 Leo	11 Lib
13 Leo	14 Lib	13 Lib	14 Sag	14 Cap	15 Pis	14 Ari	13 Tau	13 Can	13 Leo	12 Vir	14 Sco
15 Vir	16 Sco	16 Sco	17 Cap	16 Aqu	17 Ari	16 Tau	15 Gem	15 Leo	15 Vir	14 Lib	16 Sag
18 Lib	19 Sag	18 Sag	19 Aqu	19 Pis	19 Tau	19 Gem	17 Can	17 Vir	17 Lib	16 Sco	19 Cap
20 Sco	21 Cap	21 Cap	21 Pis	21 Ari	21 Gem	21 Can	19 Leo	20 Lib	20 Sco	19 Sag	21 Aqu
23 Sag	23 Aqu	23 Aqu	23 Ari	23 Tau	23 Can	23 Leo	21 Vir	23 Sco	23 Sag	21 Cap	23 Pis
25 Cap	25 Pis	25 Pis	25 Tau	25 Gem	25 Leo	24 Vir	24 Lib	25 Sag	25 Cap	24 Aqu	25 Ari
27 Aqu	27 Ari	27 Ari	27 Gem	27 Can	27 Vir	28 Lib	26 Sco	28 Cap	27 Aqu	26 Pis	28 Tau
29 Pis		29 Tau	29 Can	29 Leo	30 Lib	30 Sco	29 Sag	30 Aqu	30 Pis	28 Ari	30 Gem
31 Ari		31 Gem		31 Vir			31 Cap			30 Tau	

JAN	FEB	MAR	APR	MAY	JUN	JUL	AUG	SEP	OCT	NOV	DEC
BORN IN THE YEAR 1999											
1 Can	1 Vir	1 Vir	2 Sco	2 Sag	3 Aqu	2 Pis	1 Ari	2 Gem	1 Can	1 Vir	1 Lib
3 Leo	4 Lib	3 Lib	4 Sag	4 Cap	5 Pis	5 Ari	3 Tau	4 Can	3 Leo	4 Lib	3 Sco
5 Vir	6 Sco	6 Sco	7 Cap	7 Aqu	8 Ari	7 Tau	5 Gem	6 Leo	5 Vir	6 Sco	6 Sag
7 Lib	9 Sag	8 Sag	9 Aqu	9 Pis	10 Tau	9 Gem	7 Can	8 Vir	8 Lib	9 Sag	8 Cap
10 Sco	11 Cap	11 Cap	12 Pis	11 Ari	12 Gem	11 Can	9 Leo	10 Lib	10 Sco	11 Cap	11 Aqu
12 Sag	14 Aqu	13 Aqu	14 Ari	13 Tau	14 Can	13 Leo	12 Vir	13 Sco	12 Sag	14 Aqu	13 Pis
15 Cap	16 Pis	15 Pis	16 Tau	15 Gem	16 Leo	15 Vir	14 Lib	15 Sag	15 Cap	16 Pis	16 Ari
17 Aqu	18 Ari	17 Ari	18 Gem	17 Can	18 Vir	17 Lib	16 Sco	18 Cap	17 Aqu	18 Ari	18 Tau
19 Pis	20 Tau	19 Tau	20 Can	19 Leo	20 Lib	20 Sco	19 Sag	20 Aqu	20 Pis	21 Tau	20 Gem
22 Ari	22 Gem	21 Gem	22 Leo	21 Vir	23 Sco	22 Sag	21 Cap	22 Pis	22 Ari	23 Gem	22 Can
24 Tau	24 Can	23 Can	24 Vir	24 Lib	25 Sag	25 Cap	24 Aqu	25 Ari	24 Tau	25 Can	24 Leo
26 Gem	26 Leo	26 Leo	27 Lib	26 Sco	28 Cap	27 Aqu	26 Pis	27 Tau	26 Gem	27 Leo	26 Vir
28 Can		28 Vir	29 Sco	29 Sag	30 Aqu	30 Pis	28 Ari	29 Gem	28 Can	29 Vir	28 Lib
30 Leo		30 Lib		31 Cap			30 Tau		30 Leo		31 Sco
BORN IN THE YEAR 2000											
3 Sag	1 Cap	2 Aqu	1 Pis	3 Tau	1 Gem	2 Leo	1 Vir	2 Sco	1 Sag	3 Aqu	2 Pis
5 Cap	4 Aqu	4 Pis	3 Ari	5 Gem	3 Can	4 Vir	3 Lib	4 Sag	4 Cap	5 Pis	5 Ari
7 Aqu	6 Pis	7 Ari	5 Tau	7 Can	5 Leo	7 Lib	5 Sco	6 Cap	6 Aqu	8 Ari	7 Tau
10 P s	8 Ari	9 Tau	7 Gem	9 Leo	7 Vir	9 Sco	8 Sag	9 Aqu	9 Pis	10 Tau	9 Gem
12 A i	11 Tau	11 Gem	9 Can	11 Vir	9 Lib	11 Sag	10 Cap	11 Pis	11 Ari	12 Gem	11 Can
14 Tau	13 Gem	13 Can	11 Leo	13 Lib	12 Sco	14 Cap	13 Aqu	14 Ari	13 Tau	14 Can	13 Leo
16 Gem	15 Can	15 Leo	14 Vir	15 Sco	14 Sag	16 Aqu	15 Pis	16 Tau	16 Gem	16 Leo	15 Vir
18 Can	17 Leo	17 Vir	16 Lib	18 Sag	17 Cap	19 Pis	18 Ari	18 Gem	18 Can	18 Vir	18 Lib
20 Leo	19 Vir	20 Lib	18 Sco	20 Cap	19 Aqu	21 Ari	20 Tau	20 Can	20 Leo	20 Lib	20 Sco
23 Vir	21 Lib	22 Sco	21 Sag	23 Aqu	22 Pis	24 Tau	22 Gem	23 Leo	22 Vir	23 Sco	22 Sag
25 Li	23 Sco	24 Sag	23 Cap	25 Pis	24 Ari	26 Gem	24 Can	25 Vir	24 Lib	25 Sag	25 Cap
27 Sco	26 Sag	27 Cap	26 Aqu	28 Ari	26 Tau	28 Can	26 Leo	27 Lib	26 Sco	27 Cap	27 Aqu
29 Sag	28 Cap	29 Aqu	28 Pis	30 Tau	28 Gem	30 Leo	28 Vir	29 Sco	29 Sag	30 Aqu	30 Pis
			30 Ari		30 Can		30 Lib		31 Cap		
BORN IN THE YEAR 2001											
1 Ari	2 Gem	1 Gem	2 Leo	1 Vir	2 Sco	1 Sag	3 Aqu	1 Pis	1 Ari	2 Gem	2 Can
4 Tau	4 Can	4 Can	4 Vir	3 Lib	4 Sag	4 Cap	5 Pis	4 Ari	4 Tau	4 Can	4 Leo
6 Gem	6 Leo	6 Leo	6 Lib	6 Sco	7 Cap	6 Aqu	8 Ari	6 Tau	6 Gem	7 Leo	6 Vir
8 Can	8 Vir	9 Vir	8 Sco	8 Sag	9 Aqu	9 Pis	10 Tau	9 Gem	8 Can	9 Vir	8 Lib
10 Leo	10 Lib	10 Lib	10 Sag	10 Cap	11 Pis	11 Ari	12 Gem	11 Can	10 Leo	11 Lib	10 Sco
12 Vir	12 Sco	12 Sco	13 Cap	13 Aqu	14 Ari	14 Tau	15 Can	13 Leo	13 Vir	13 Sco	12 Sag
14 Lib	15 Sag	14 Sag	15 Aqu	15 Pis	16 Tau	16 Can	17 Leo	15 Vir	15 Lib	15 Sag	15 Cap
16 Sco	17 Cap	16 Cap	18 Pis	18 Ari	19 Gem	18 Can	19 Vir	17 Lib	17 Sco	17 Cap	17 Aqu
18 Sag	20 Agu	19 Aqu	20 Ari	20 Tau	21 Can	20 Leo	21 Lib	19 Sco	19 Sag	20 Aqu	20 Pis
21 Cap	22 Pis	22 Pis	23 Tau	22 Gem	23 Leo	22 Vir	23 Sco	21 Sag	21 Cap	22 Pis	22 Ari
23 Aqu	25 Ari	24 Ari	25 Gem	24 Can	25 Vir	24 Lib	25 Sag	23 Cap	23 Aqu	25 Ari	25 Tau
26 Pis	27 Tau	26 Tau	27 Can	27 Leo	27 Lib	26 Sco	27 Cap	26 Aqu	26 Pis	27 Tau	27 Gem
28 Ari		29 Gem	29 Leo	29 Vir	29 Sco	29 Sag	30 Aqu	28 Pis	28 Ari	30 Gem	29 Can
31 Tau		31 Can		31 Lib		31 Cap			31 Tau		31 Leo
BORN IN THE YEAR 2002											
2 Vir	1 Lib	2 Sco	1 Sag	2 Aqu	1 Pis	1 Ari	2 Gem	1 Can	1 Leo	1 Lib	1 Sco
4 Lib	3 Sco	4 Sag	3 Cap	5 Pis	4 Ari	4 Tau	5 Can	3 Leo	3 Vir	3 Sco	3 Sag
6 Sco	5 Sag	6 Cap	5 Aqu	7 Ari	6 Tau	6 Gem	7 Leo	5 Vir	5 Lib	5 Sag	5 Cap
9 Sag	7 Cap	9 Aqu	8 Pis	10 Tau	9 Gem	8 Can	9 Vir	7 Lib	7 Sco	7 Cap	7 Aqu
11 Cap	10 Aqu	11 Pis	10 Ari	12 Gem	11 Can	11 Leo	11 Lib	9 Sco	9 Sag	10 Aqu	9 Pis
13 Aqu	12 Pis	14 Ari	13 Tau	15 Can	14 Leo	13 Vir	13 Sco	12 Sag	11 Cap	12 Pis	12 Ari
16 Pis	15 Ari	16 Tau	15 Gem	17 Leo	16 Vir	15 Lib	15 Sag	14 Cap	13 Aqu	15 Ari	14 Tau
18 Ari	17 Tau	19 Gem	18 Can	19 Vir	18 Lib	17 Sco	18 Cap	16 Aqu	16 Pis	17 Tau	17 Gem
21 Tau	20 Gem	21 Can	20 Leo	21 Lib	20 Sco	19 Sag	20 Aqu	19 Pis	18 Ari	20 Gem	19 Can
23 Gem	22 Can	24 Leo	22 Vir	23 Sco	22 Sag	22 Cap	22 Pis	21 Ari	21 Tau	22 Can	22 Leo
26 Can	24 Leo	26 Vir	24 Lib	25 Sag	24 Cap	24 Aqu	25 Ari	24 Tau	23 Gem	24 Leo	24 Vir
28 Leo	26 Vir	28 Lib	26 Sco	28 Cap	26 Pis	27 Tau	26 Gem	26 Can	27 Vir	26 Lib	
30 Vir	28 Lib	30 Sco	28 Sag	30 Aqu	29 Pis	28 Ari	30 Gem	29 Can	28 Leo	29 Lib	28 Sco
			30 Sag				31 Tau			30 Vir	30 Sag

	JAN	FEB	MAR	APR	MAY	JUN	JUL	AUG	SEP	OCT	NOV	DEC
BORN IN THE YEAR 2003												
	1 Cap	2 Pis	1 Pis	3 Tau	2 Gem	1 Can	1 Leo	2 Lib	2 Sag	1 Cap	2 Pis	2 Ari
	3 Aqu	5 Ari	4 Ari	5 Gem	5 Can	4 Leo	3 Vir	4 Sco	4 Cap	4 Aqu	5 Ari	4 Tau
	6 Pis	7 Tau	6 Tau	8 Can	7 Leo	6 Vir	5 Lib	6 Sag	6 Aqu	6 Pis	7 Tau	7 Gem
	8 Ari	10 Gem	9 Gem	10 Leo	10 Vir	8 Lib	7 Sco	8 Cap	9 Pis	8 Ari	10 Gem	9 Can
	11 Tau	12 Can	11 Can	12 Vir	12 Lib	10 Sco	10 Sag	10 Aqu	11 Ari	11 Tau	12 Can	12 Leo
	13 Gem	14 Leo	14 Leo	14 Lib	14 Sco	12 Sag	12 Pis	13 Pis	13 Tau	13 Gem	15 Leo	14 Vir
	16 Can	16 Vir	16 Vir	16 Sco	16 Sag	15 Ari	14 Aqu	15 Ari	16 Gem	16 Can	17 Vir	16 Lib
	18 Leo	18 Lib	18 Lib	18 Sag	18 Cap	16 Aqu	16 Pis	17 Tau	18 Can	18 Leo	19 Lib	19 Sco
	20 Vir	21 Sco	20 Sco	20 Cap	20 Aqu	19 Pis	18 Ari	20 Gem	21 Leo	21 Vir	21 Sco	21 Sag
	22 Lib	23 Sag	22 Sag	22 Pis	22 Pis	21 Ari	21 Tau	22 Can	23 Vir	23 Lib	23 Sag	23 Cap
	24 Sco	25 Cap	24 Cap	25 Pis	25 Ari	23 Tau	23 Gem	24 Leo	25 Lib	25 Sco	25 Cap	25 Aqu
	26 Sag	27 Aqu	26 Aqu	27 Ari	27 Tau	26 Gem	26 Can	27 Vir	27 Sco	27 Sag	27 Aqu	27 Pis
	29 Cap		29 Pis	30 Tau	30 Gem	28 Can	28 Leo	29 Lib	29 Cap	29 Cap	29 Pis	29 Ari
	31 Aqu		31 Ari				30 Vir	31 Sco		31 Aqu		
BORN IN THE YEAR 2004												
	1 Tau	2 Can	3 Leo	1 Vir	1 Lib	2 Sag	1 Cap	1 Pis	2 Tau	2 Gem	1 Can	1 Leo
	3 Gem	4 Leo	5 Vir	4 Lib	3 Sco	4 Cap	3 Aqu	4 Ari	5 Gem	5 Can	3 Leo	3 Vir
	6 Can	7 Vir	7 Lib	6 Sco	5 Sag	6 Aqu	5 Pis	6 Tau	7 Can	7 Leo	6 Vir	6 Lib
	8 Leo	9 Lib	9 Sco	9 Sag	7 Cap	8 Pis	7 Ari	8 Gem	10 Leo	10 Vir	8 Lib	8 Sco
	10 Vir	11 Sco	12 Sag	10 Cap	9 Aqu	10 Ari	10 Tau	11 Can	12 Vir	12 Lib	10 Sco	10 Sag
	13 Lib	13 Sag	14 Cap	12 Aqu	11 Pis	12 Tau	12 Gem	13 Leo	14 Lib	14 Sco	13 Sag	12 Cap
	15 Sco	15 Cap	16 Aqu	14 Pis	14 Ari	15 Gem	15 Can	16 Vir	17 Sco	15 Sag	15 Cap	14 Aqu
	17 Sag	17 Aqu	18 Pis	16 Ari	16 Tau	17 Can	17 Leo	18 Lib	19 Sag	18 Cap	17 Aqu	16 Pis
	19 Cap	20 Pis	20 Ari	19 Tau	19 Gem	20 Leo	20 Vir	20 Sco	21 Cap	20 Aqu	19 Pis	18 Ari
	21 Aqu	22 Ari	23 Tau	21 Gem	21 Can	22 Vir	22 Lib	23 Sag	23 Aqu	23 Pis	21 Ari	21 Tau
	23 Pis	24 Tau	25 Gem	24 Can	24 Leo	25 Lib	24 Sco	25 Cap	25 Pis	25 Ari	23 Tau	23 Gem
	25 Ari	27 Gem	28 Can	26 Leo	26 Vir	27 Sco	27 Sag	28 Aqu	27 Ari	27 Tau	26 Gem	25 Can
	28 Tau	29 Can	30 Leo	29 Vir	28 Lib	29 Sag	29 Cap	29 Pis	29 Tau	29 Gem	28 Can	28 Leo
	30 Gem				31 Sco		30 Aqu	31 Ari				31 Vir
BORN IN THE YEAR 2005												
	2 Lib	1 Sag	2 Sag	3 Aqu	2 Pis	3 Tau	2 Gem	1 Can	2 Vir	2 Lib	1 Sco	2 Cap
	4 Sco	3 Cap	4 Cap	5 Pis	4 Ari	5 Gem	5 Can	3 Leo	5 Lib	4 Sco	3 Sag	4 Aqu
	6 Sag	5 Cap	6 Aqu	7 Ari	6 Tau	7 Can	7 Leo	6 Vir	7 Sco	7 Sag	5 Cap	7 Pis
	8 Cap	7 Aqu	8 Pis	9 Tau	9 Gem	10 Leo	10 Vir	8 Lib	9 Sag	9 Cap	7 Aqu	9 Ari
	10 Aqu	9 Pis	10 Ari	11 Gem	11 Can	12 Vir	12 Lib	11 Sco	12 Cap	11 Aqu	9 Pis	11 Tau
	12 Pis	11 Ari	13 Tau	14 Can	14 Leo	15 Lib	15 Sco	13 Sag	14 Aqu	13 Pis	11 Ari	13 Gem
	15 Ari	13 Tau	15 Gem	16 Leo	16 Vir	17 Sco	17 Sag	15 Cap	16 Pis	15 Ari	14 Tau	15 Can
	17 Tau	16 Gem	17 Can	19 Vir	18 Lib	19 Sag	19 Cap	18 Aqu	18 Ari	17 Tau	16 Gem	18 Leo
	19 Gem	18 Can	20 Leo	21 Lib	21 Sco	21 Cap	21 Aqu	19 Pis	20 Tau	19 Gem	18 Can	20 Vir
	22 Can	21 Leo	22 Vir	23 Sco	23 Sag	23 Aqu	23 Pis	21 Ari	22 Gem	22 Can	21 Leo	23 Lib
	24 Leo	23 Vir	25 Lib	26 Sag	25 Cap	25 Pis	25 Ari	23 Tau	24 Can	24 Leo	23 Vir	25 Sco
	27 Vir	25 Lib	27 Sco	28 Cap	27 Aqu	28 Ari	27 Tau	26 Gem	27 Leo	27 Vir	26 Lib	28 Sag
	29 Lib	28 Sco	29 Sag	30 Aqu	29 Pis	30 Tau	30 Gem	28 Can	29 Vir	29 Lib	28 Sco	30 Cap
			31 Cap		31 Ari			31 Leo			30 Sag	
BORN IN THE YEAR 2006												
	1 Aqu	1 Ari	1 Ari	1 Gem	1 Can	2 Vir	2 Lib	1 Sco	2 Cap	1 Aqu	2 Ari	1 Tau
	3 Pis	3 Tau	3 Tau	4 Can	3 Leo	5 Lib	5 Sco	3 Sag	4 Aqu	3 Pis	4 Tau	3 Gem
	5 Ari	6 Gem	5 Gem	6 Leo	6 Vir	7 Sco	7 Sag	6 Cap	6 Pis	6 Ari	6 Gem	6 Can
	7 Tau	8 Can	7 Can	9 Vir	8 Lib	10 Sag	10 Cap	8 Aqu	8 Ari	8 Tau	8 Can	8 Leo
	9 Gem	10 Leo	10 Leo	11 Lib	11 Sco	12 Cap	12 Aqu	10 Pis	10 Tau	10 Gem	10 Leo	10 Vir
	12 Can	13 Vir	12 Vir	14 Sco	13 Sag	14 Aqu	14 Pis	12 Ari	12 Gem	12 Can	13 Vir	13 Lib
	14 Leo	16 Lib	15 Lib	16 Sag	15 Cap	16 Pis	16 Ari	14 Tau	14 Can	14 Leo	15 Lib	15 Sco
	17 Vir	18 Sco	17 Sco	18 Cap	18 Aqu	18 Ari	17 Tau	16 Gem	17 Leo	18 Sco	18 Sag	18 Sag
	19 Lib	20 Sag	20 Sag	20 Aqu	20 Pis	20 Tau	20 Gem	20 Leo	19 Vir	19 Lib	20 Sag	20 Cap
	22 Sco	23 Cap	22 Cap	22 Pis	22 Ari	22 Gem	22 Can	21 Leo	22 Lib	22 Sco	23 Cap	22 Aqu
	24 Sag	25 Aqu	24 Aqu	24 Ari	24 Tau	25 Can	24 Leo	23 Vir	24 Sco	24 Sag	25 Aqu	24 Pis
	26 Cap	27 Pis	26 Pis	27 Tau	27 Gem	27 Leo	27 Vir	26 Lib	27 Sag	26 Cap	27 Pis	27 Ari
	28 Aqu		28 Ari	28 Can	29 Can	29 Vir	29 Lib	28 Sco	29 Aqu	29 Aqu	29 Ari	29 Tau
	30 Pis		30 Tau		31 Leo		31 Sag			31 Pis		31 Gem

WHAT YOUR MOON SIGN SAYS ABOUT YOU

Now that you know your Moon sign, read on to learn more about your emotional nature and your basic inner needs.

MOON IN ARIES

You have an emotional need to be first. And you want to be first *now* – there's no time to waste. Brimming with enthusiasm and energy, you love to keep busy and find waiting difficult. Remember to open up and talk to those closest to you about your feelings – they can help you to slow down and deal with any difficult emotions as they arise.

MOON IN TAURUS

You love to be surrounded by beautiful possessions and enjoy food and clothes that make you feel good – you have a need for comfort. Familiarity and routine are important to you, and you don't deal well with sudden change. That stubborn streak means you're able to stand up for yourself and protect your own interests, just remember to relax once in a while and try new things.

MOON IN GEMINI

Self-expression is one of your driving forces with this mix. Talking, drawing, writing – you simply have to communicate your feelings. And you love to listen to other peoples' ideas, too. To feed your curious intellect, you've probably got a tower of books and magazines at your bedside. Just don't forget to exercise your body as well as your mind.

MOON IN CANCER

You were born to nurture others – whether that's through baking them a cake or being at the end of the phone when they need your reassuring words. Family is hugely important to you, and you want to feel loved and secure. Being honest about this and accepting your wonderfully sensitive and emotional nature will help you find inner peace.

MOON IN LEO

You have an emotional need to be admired – all you really want is for everyone to love you. Your kind heart and generosity towards your friends and family means you are usually surrounded by others, and the attention you crave is easily won. When things don't go your way, you have a tendency to be dramatic – don't let your pride stop you from asking for help when you need it.

MOON IN VIRGO

You are a gentle soul and appreciate the simple things in life. Helping others in small ways makes you feel needed, secure and purposeful. A clean and tidy environment is a must, and everything has to be in its proper place. Learning not to fuss when something isn't perfect is a challenge – look for useful ways to keep your practical nature busy and happiness will follow.

MOON IN LIBRA

Close bonds are everything to you – you find strength and stability in your relationships with others. Your need for balance and harmony means you are an excellent peacemaker, skilled at helping people to see and understand another's perspective. Remember to feed your love of beauty with regular trips to art galleries and picturesque places.

MOON IN SCORPIO

Deep and emotionally intense, you need to trust those close to you with your innermost thoughts and desires. All or nothing, you have incredible intuition and can see right to the heart of people. Finding one or two close friends who you can really open up to and be honest with about your feelings is important for your happiness. When this happens, your inner strength is unmatched.

MOON IN SAGITTARIUS

Your need for freedom and space is overwhelming, but when you achieve it, you are bright, breezy and filled with a zest for life. Always on the lookout for new things to try and people to meet, your energy and enthusiasm lifts the spirits of those around you. Planning is not your strong suit; you prefer to go with the flow and see where it takes you – preferably somewhere fun and interesting!

MOON IN CAPRICORN

Ambitious and practical, you want to work hard and achieve results. You are conscientious and naturally organized, with a clear picture of what you want and how you intend to get there. Remember to take time to kick back and relax – the strong front you present to those around you can hide your more sensitive side. Letting go occasionally isn't a sign of weakness.

MOON IN AQUARIUS

Your desire to be unique and unusual is powerful, and you need the space and freedom to be yourself. Emotionally detached, you are happily independent and have an ability to see the bigger picture. Try not to lose touch with those closest to you – life is full of ups and downs, and friends and family can offer valuable support through tougher times.

MOON IN PISCES

Dreamy and intuitive, your sensitive nature is highly attuned to the feelings of others. Be careful to steer clear of negative people – you're likely to absorb their vibes, and they will bring you down. It's important you learn how to take care of yourself when you feel overwhelmed emotionally. Escaping into a good book or listening to your favourite music can be a great way to re-set.

ELEMENTS

YOUR ELEMENTAL TYPE

Fire, Earth, Air, Water – in ancient times these were thought to contain everything that existed on Earth. Today that's no longer the case, but there's no denying their powerful effect on people's lives. Think of the heat from the Sun, the way earth is used to grow food, the water you consume, the air that you breathe. And like so much in astrology, each element has two sides. You drink water and rain helps plants to grow, but the force of a tsunami can wreak havoc and destruction. You have all four elements within you, but one or more of them will stand out. You could be a single type, or a mix of two or three. Your elemental type says a lot about you and those you interact with. When you meet someone you feel naturally comfortable with, it's often because you are elementally compatible.

IN YOUR ELEMENT

Oriented towards what is real, Virgos love to use knowledge in a practical way. The most adaptable of all the Earth signs, you look for logical answers to problems and are good at making the tough decisions no one else wants to. Cool-headed and hard-working, you concentrate on the job at hand without fuss. But if plans fall through or something can't be explained, you can feel jittery.

 ### EARTH WITH FIRE

Not ideally compatible, as Earth extinguishes Fire, while 'scorched Earth' is sterile and unproductive. Still, Fire can get you going, energizing you with its passion and intensity, while you can slow Fire down, acting as a grounding force.

 ### EARTH WITH EARTH

Stable and peaceful, you are very compatible, reinforcing each other's strengths. Watch out you don't get stuck in the same routine or focus so much on the practical side of things you forget to let loose and have some fun.

 ### EARTH WITH AIR

Not an ideal mix. Air wants excitement rather than stability, and Earth can feel irritated by Air's flightiness. You do challenge each other to think differently and see things from a new perspective, but ultimately Earth can find Air exhausting.

 ### EARTH WITH WATER

Comfortable and secure, you work wonderfully together, each helping the other to reach their potential. You are Water's rock, grounding them emotionally and helping them to get things done, while Water refreshes and enlivens you.

THE MISSING PIECE

How dominant Earth is within you depends on the influence of the other elements in your chart – ideally all four would be represented. Sometimes a lack of a particular element can cause an imbalance, making you feel rundown or stressed. The best way to counteract this is to tune in to the missing element and reharmonize yourself. Try the simple exercise below to get back in touch with any elements you're missing.

1. First, take a look at the Zodiac signs and their elements.

Fire: Aries, Leo, Sagittarius

Earth: Taurus, Virgo, Capricorn

Air: Gemini, Libra, Aquarius

Water: Cancer, Scorpio, Pisces

2. Now circle Earth, as this is the element that represents your Sun sign. You're certain to have some of this element. Then do the same for your Moon sign and your Ascendant, circling the element associated with each.

3. Looking at the list, there should be one or more elements you haven't circled.

Fire – not enough Fire can leave you lacking in energy and motivation. You want to be more assertive and prepared to take the lead.

Air – Air will help you to communicate better, feel more sociable and lift your spirits. Use it to boost your curiosity and sharpen your wits.

Water – with Water missing you may struggle to get in touch with your emotions or worry you're being insensitive. You're looking to express yourself, to feel more creative and inspired.

4. Choose the element you would like to tune in to, whichever one you feel might benefit you. Then pick one of the ideas from the lists below. If Fire is missing, you could turn your face to the sun and soak up its warmth. If it's Water, you could try a soak in the bath. You can use this exercise whenever you feel out of balance.

FIRE

Sunbathe
Toast marshmallows
Watch fireworks
Host a barbecue
Meditate on a candle flame
Catch the sunrise
Go stargazing

AIR

Fly a kite
Watch clouds go by
Blow bubbles
Feel the breeze
Breathe deep
Play with a balloon
Chase butterflies

WATER

Spend a day at the beach
Splash in a puddle
Sit by a fountain
Walk in the rain
Catch a wave
Snorkel

WE'RE ALL IN THIS TOGETHER

When so much in your life is changing, your relationships with your parents can become even more important. If you're lucky, you get on well with yours, but even the most harmonious relationships can come under strain during the teenage years. How can astrology help? It can remind you that parents are people, too. They might not get everything right, but hopefully you believe that they have your best interests at heart. Learning more about who they are, why they do things and how you relate to them can make it easier for all of you to move forwards together.

MOTHER MOON

The Moon sign you are born with can tell you a lot about how you see and treat your mother. This is because your Moon sign represents your emotional needs – what you need to feel safe and secure – and these are most often fulfilled by your mother. How you react to her can make a big difference to the way she behaves around you. If you are visibly upset by certain things she does, she is likely to change her behaviour the next time around. If you react with happiness and delight, she is more likely to repeat them.

Here's how you see your mother according to your Moon sign . . .

ARIES

You view your mother as strong, honest and forthright. Sometimes, especially when she doesn't agree with your plans, this can make you feel as though she's taking over. Try not to push back too strongly, and remember she has your interests at heart.

TAURUS

You like to feel your mother is looking after all of your everyday needs and is dependable and reliable. Don't judge her too harshly if she doesn't always live up to your expectations – providing for others is often a careful balancing act, and she is likely doing her best.

GEMINI

Flighty and impulsive, you need your mother to give you the freedom to be yourself and make your own mistakes. Space and independence often have to be earned, though – what could you do to show her you're capable and trustworthy?

CANCER

Your longing for your mother's emotional attention can give you a wonderful bond and connection. However, the slightest hint of rejection from her can wound you deeply. Try not to take her reactions personally – it's okay for her to make choices and have goals that differ from yours.

LEO

You want to enjoy an open, honest relationship with your mother, where both of you say what you mean. Underlying this candour is a need for assurance and acceptance – when you feel vulnerable, be brave and explain to her how you feel.

VIRGO

You are aware of who gives what in your emotional relationship with your mother, and occasionally this can make you feel that she isn't there for you. Viewing her actions as 'different' rather than 'wrong' will help you to trust she is doing what she thinks is right.

LIBRA

You need your mother to recognize your emotional needs as valid and important. Try not to spend too much time putting others first – your relationship will flourish when you both accept the roles you play.

SCORPIO

You want your mother to respect your emotional boundaries and allow you alone-time when you need it. The trust between you can be intense and unconditional, so much so you may have to remind her to step back occasionally.

SAGITTARIUS

Upbeat and curious, your relationship works best when your mother is inspiring and encouraging, giving you the emotional freedom you need to expand your horizons. It's fine to chase independence, as long as you respect your mother's desire to give you roots.

CAPRICORN

You empathize strongly with your mother's feelings, so when she's struggling, this can make you feel it's your fault. Learn to let go of this guilt – it's unintentional and unhelpful. Instead, recognize how much you need each other's emotional support and encouragement.

AQUARIUS

You're not sure your mother's attempts to guide you are always necessary, and don't like to burden her with your problems. Asking for help and talking things through might be more useful than you imagine and can bring you closer together at the same time.

PISCES

Your mother's high expectations have made you stronger emotionally, even though there are times when you just want to feel like a child and let her take care of everything. Taking responsibility can be tough; don't be afraid to speak up when you need support.

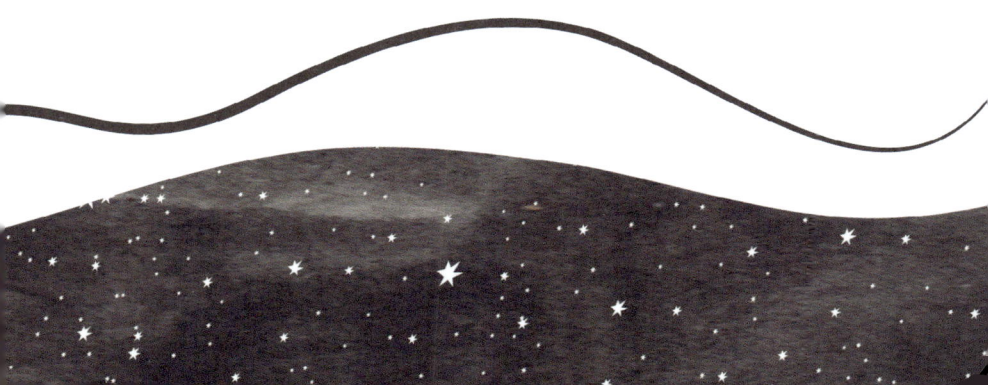

HOW YOU SEE YOUR FATHER

Just as your Moon sign gives you an indication of how you see your mother, or whoever plays that nurturing role in your life, your Sun sign can reveal the way you view your father, or the caregiver who is most involved with discipline. Your relationship with this person is built over time. For girls, it can have a strong bearing on how you view any future romantic relationships, whereas boys will either rebel or identify with these traits.

With your Virgo Sun sign, you think your father happily takes control of the everyday routines. He's the one who pops his head around the bedroom door to check you've cleaned your teeth or picked up the laundry off the floor. When you hang out together, there's the bonus that he loves to help you with homework.

Now read on to find out how your father's Sun sign affects your relationship . . .

Your father's Sun sign will play a significant part in how you relate to him, and it can help you to understand why he acts the way he does – however infuriating it may sometimes seem!

ARIES

Impulsive and energetic, your dad's lack of organization can drive you up the wall. Luckily, you're orderly enough for the both of you. Over time, the two of you are likely to find a happy balance in your relationship.

TAURUS

Your strong father likes to encourage you to have confidence and show you how to calm any anxieties. He can be on the strict side, but there's also love, which is often demonstrated through surprise gifts.

GEMINI

Mercury, the planet of communication, rules both of your signs, although it doesn't always lead to harmony. You also share a critical streak, and when that collides, there can be fireworks. Underlying it, though, is a deep love for each other.

CANCER

This pairing means that you have a shared sixth sense. Each of you can pick up on the other's emotions without a word being spoken. Try to remember to talk about any big issues, however, or wires could get crossed.

LEO

There is often a deep devotion and respect between the two of you that other families can only dream about. Your dad's showiness doesn't overshadow you thanks to your strong sense of self and quiet confidence.

VIRGO

As fellow Earth signs, you share a practical attitude to life. Emotional heart-to-hearts tend not to be your thing, and you might prefer to spend time together on tasks with a clear result at the end, be that baking or DIY.

LIBRA

This is a mutually beneficial mix. Your dad is focused on developing your appreciation of the arts and insists on regular gallery visits, while you love helping out in practical ways around the house.

SCORPIO

You are curious but in different ways. You prefer to observe from the sidelines, whereas your father relies on instinct and intuition. You could both benefit from lightening up – put your worries to one side occasionally and just enjoy the ride.

SAGITTARIUS

If anyone is looking for you two, they'll probably find you huddled at the laptop, searching for information. You both soak up knowledge like a sponge and may even consider applying for a TV quiz show, cheering each other on.

CAPRICORN

Although you are both Earth signs – often known for their honesty – you can find it difficult to express your feelings to each other. Exploring things you have in common, a love of football, for example, can point you in the right direction.

AQUARIUS

When your kind natures combine, it's likely you'll volunteer for every charitable event going. While this is admirable, be careful to include any siblings or there could be some hurt feelings closer to home.

PISCES

This combination can lead to strong flights of fancy into the realms of imagination. And while it can be a lovely place to be, you'll both need to remember to come back down to Earth – sometimes with a bump.

Best of
FRIENDS

FRIENDS FOR LIFE

Friends play an essential role in your happiness. They can help you to move forwards when times are tough, see things from a new perspective and encourage you just to have fun. Every good friend you make has different qualities that will influence you and allow you to make more of your potential. A friend might show you it can be better to hold back when all you want to do is rush in, motivate you to stick with that project right to the end or inspire you to see an obstacle as a challenge. And astrology can be a great way to highlight those characteristics you're looking for in a friend. It can also tell you more about the type of friend you make for others.

WHAT KIND OF FRIEND ARE YOU?

You can be shy and self-conscious, which can get in the way of making new acquaintances, but once you feel secure within a friendship, your charming and kind side quickly shines through. You're often the one people turn to in times of trouble, both for your tenderness and the well-thought-out advice you give. You like to be organized, so prefer to make plans well in advance and expect your friends to stick to them.

Strengths: *Warm, modest, smart*
Weakness: *Shy, serious, overly critical*
Friendship style: *Fixer, good communicator, reliable*

IF YOUR BEST FRIEND IS . . .

ARIES

Aries make friends easily. They're willing to help you achieve your goals, they see the best in you and they're happy to take risks for you, too. They love to be someone's best friend and can find it difficult to feel second to anyone else. They are always on the lookout for new, super-fun adventures and are happy to take you along for the ride. They have a knack of bringing people from all walks of life together.

Strengths: *Loyal, generous, fun-loving*
Weaknesses: *Insensitive, demanding, petulant*
Friendship style: *Busy, fun, warm*

TAURUS

Considerate and charming, Taurus friends often have a talent for giving good advice. They like to take their time and allow friendships to develop slowly, but once you become close they treat you as a member of their family. As an Earth sign, they are dependable and grounded, and they make wonderful lifelong friends. Bear in mind they can place too much importance on material possessions, even judging others based on their wealth.

Strengths: *Caring, faithful, trustworthy*
Weaknesses: *Judgmental, stubborn, materialistic*
Friendship style: *Helpful, sweet, self-assured*

GEMINI

You'll need lots of energy to keep up with a Gemini friend. They love to have fun, do crazy things and always have a story to tell. They'll make you laugh, but they can sometimes get a little carried away, perhaps exaggerating tales of their adventures in their effort to entertain you. They can be a bit gossipy, but they're not malicious. They're good listeners and will make you feel great, giving you lots of compliments – and always genuine ones, too.

Strengths: *Intelligent, energetic, fearless*
Weaknesses: *Impatient, easily bored, gossipy*
Friendship style: *Good listener, witty, spontaneous*

CANCER

Once you form a close connection with Cancer, you have a friend who has your back. They're considerate and like nothing better than to make you feel happy. Watch out though; they're deeply emotional, which means that if you argue – even over something small – you'll have to work hard to patch things up again.

Strengths: *Loving, caring, intuitive*
Weaknesses: *Unforgiving, anxious, sensitive*
Friendship style: *Warm, affectionate, protective*

LEO

As long as you don't expect too much from a Leo friend, you're in for a treat. Outgoing, confident and full of energy, they thrive on social occasions and love to be the life and soul of a party, making people laugh and being admired. They're good at bringing people together and are in high demand, so you won't always have them to yourself, but if you can tie them down you'll have some great quality one-on-one time.

Strengths: *Honest, brave, positive*
Weaknesses: *Arrogant, self-centred, proud*
Friendship style: *Supportive, cheerful, humorous*

LIBRA

You can rely on your Libra friend to tell you how it is. They have a refreshing honesty, but they also have a diplomatic way of sparing your feelings. They love spending time with you and like nothing better than a chat (especially if they're the one doing the talking!). They can always see both sides, so if there's a disagreement it won't be for long.

Strengths: *Diplomatic, honest, sociable*
Weaknesses: *Indecisive, people pleaser, chatterbox*
Friendship style: *Laid-back, devoted, forgiving*

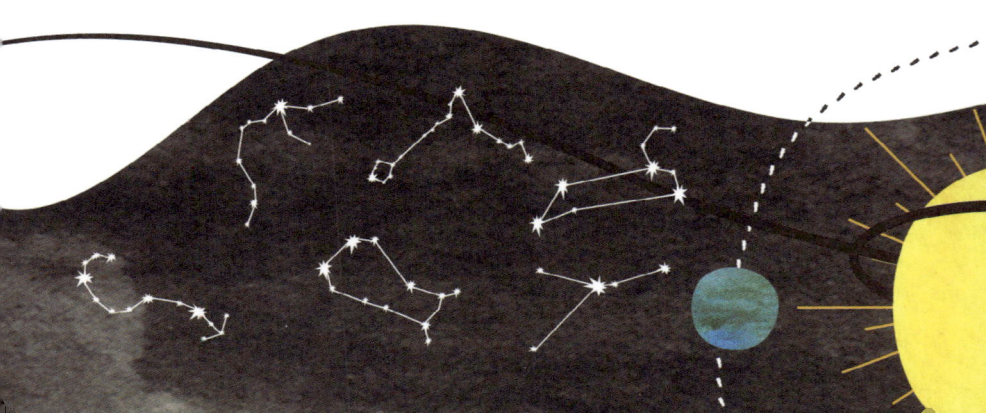

SCORPIO

It's an honour to be a Scorpio's best friend. They're selective, so they don't always have many, but the friendships they do make will be really special. Once you've cemented your friendship, they'll open their inner circle to you and will want to spend lots of time together. In return, they'll expect 100 per cent loyalty and might not take it well if you let them down, so tread carefully.

Strengths: *Passionate, hospitable, perceptive*
Weaknesses: *Guarded, jealous, suspicious*
Friendship style: *Intense, selective, loyal*

SAGITTARIUS

Sagittarius are low-maintenance friends. Easy-going, positive and happy-go-lucky, they're up for anything. If you fancy an adventure, give them a call, but don't expect too much of them feelings-wise. Their friendship circle is wide and diverse, so you'll get to meet lots of interesting people, but they are easily bored and can struggle with emotional closeness. On the plus side, they won't put too many demands on you, so give them some space and enjoy the ride.

Strengths: *Adventurous, positive, open-minded*
Weaknesses: *Impatient, insensitive, easily bored*
Friendship style: *Generous, undemanding, never dull*

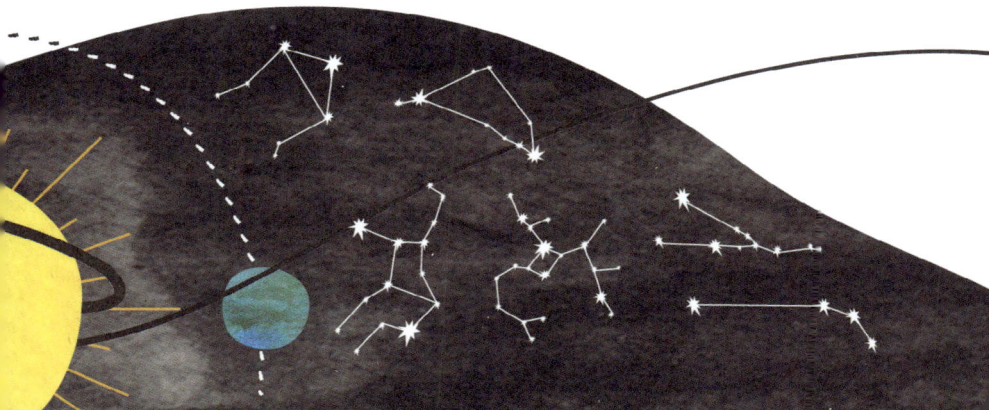

CAPRICORN

You might have to put in some groundwork, but once you've cracked the seemingly aloof exterior of a Capricorn you'll have yourself a genuine, warm, loving and faithful friend. They'll show you complete devotion, through the good times and the bad. They're thoughtful and sensible and will know when to call it a night, but they will often surprise you with their sly sense of humour. They love to make you smile.

Strengths: *Responsible, supportive, faithful*
Weaknesses: *Condescending, standoffish, serious*
Friendship style: *Thoughtful, rational, work hard/play hard*

AQUARIUS

You'll have to share your Aquarius best friend – they'll probably flit in and out of lots of other friendships, too – but rest assured they've got your back and w ll go to the ends of the earth for you. They'll bring plenty of excitement and fun into your world, but they also treasure their alone time, so don't put too many demands on them. They'll never pass judgment on you, no matter what you co.

Strengths: *Tolerant, independent, energetic*
Weaknesses: *Easily bored, rebellious, forgetful*
Friendship style: *Fun, exciting, unpredictable*

PISCES

A Pisces friend is a great listener who is sympathetic and caring and will always make time for you. They're the perfect friend if you need a shoulder to cry on, but they can sometimes get too emotionally involved. If there is any discord in your friendship, they are quick to blame themselves. Reassure them and let them know it's not their fault and you'll soon win back their love and support.

Strengths: *Loving, caring, good listener*
Weaknesses: *Sensitive, self-pitying, insecure*
Friendship style: *Supportive, sympathetic, selfless*

Your BIRTHDAY log

List the birthdays of your family and friends and discover their Sun signs

ARIES
March 21–April 20

Passionate, energetic, impulsive

TAURUS
April 21–May 21

Steady, tenacious, trustworthy

GEMINI

May 22–June 21

Intelligent, outgoing, witty

CANCER
June 22–July 22

Caring, home-loving, affectionate

LEO

July 23–August 23

Loud, big-hearted, fun

VIRGO

August 24–September 22

Organized, modest, responsible

LIBRA

September 23–October 22

Charming, creative, graceful

SCORPIO

October 23–November 21

Powerful, mysterious, magnetic

SAGITTARIUS
November 22–December 21

Adventurous, optimistic, lucky

CAPRICORN

December 22–January 20

Ambitious, dedicated, serious

AQUARIUS

January 21–February 19

Eccentric, independent, imaginative

PISCES

February 20–March 20

Dreamy, sensitive, compassionate

WHY OPPOSITES REALLY DO ATTRACT

The sign opposite your Ascendant (your Rising sign) on your birth chart reveals who you will attract, and who will attract you. Known as your Descendant, it's the constellation that was setting on the Western horizon at the moment and place you were born.

This sign is everything you are not – a kind of mirror image, or two sides of the same coin.

Yet, strangely, you are often drawn to the qualities of this sign over and over again in the people you meet. It's possible that these characteristics are ones you feel you lack yourself, and you sense that the other person can fill in what's missing. Sometimes it really is true that opposites attract!

Ascendant	Descendant
Aries	Libra
Taurus	Scorpio
Gemini	Sagittarius
Cancer	Capricorn
Leo	Aquarius
Virgo	Pisces
Libra	Aries
Scorpio	Taurus
Sagittarius	Gemini
Capricorn	Cancer
Aquarius	Leo
Pisces	Virgo

WHAT DO YOU LOOK FOR?

Once you've matched up your Ascendant with your Descendant from the list on the previous page, you can get to know the qualities that are most likely to attract you. You can use this information whether you're thinking about romance or friendship.

LIBRA DESCENDANT

You're looking for balance and harmony in your relationship, with someone who makes you feel interesting and important. You want to be listened to and value the ability to compromise. Gentleness and sensitivity are the qualities you're searching for.

SCORPIO DESCENDANT

You want an intense, passionate relationship with someone who will welcome you wholeheartedly into their world and want to spend lots of time with you. You are attracted to someone who will take control, but who will also look out for you and protect you.

SAGITTARIUS DESCENDANT

Adventure and fun are what you crave when it comes to love. You want someone open-minded who will accept you for who you are. You need to be given plenty of space to breathe and not be stifled by too many demands.

CAPRICORN DESCENDANT

You seek total dedication and devotion from those you love. You're happy to take your time and let a relationship develop naturally, and aren't put off by someone who appears cool or guarded. You like a cheeky sense of humour, too.

AQUARIUS DESCENDANT

You are attracted to someone who is independent and has a full life outside of your relationship, although you want to know that if push comes to shove, they will be right there for you. You like to be kept on your toes.

PISCES DESCENDANT

You're not afraid of a deep relationship with someone who wears their heart on their sleeve. You want to be cared for, emotionally supported and loved unconditionally. You want to be the centre of someone's world.

ARIES DESCENDANT

You like someone to spar with and who lets you have your own way, but is still strong enough to put their foot down when the gravity of the situation demands it. You will need to respect your partner's strength, bravery and integrity.

TAURUS DESCENDANT

Stability and reliability are high on your list of priorities when it comes to forming relationships. You dislike chaos and are drawn to people who you know won't surprise or disappoint you. Instead you want a partnership that's grounded and safe.

GEMINI DESCENDANT

You're attracted to someone who is spontaneous and fearless, and who can keep you entertained. You're likely to fall for someone who makes you feel super-special and is quick to recognize your achievements and boost your confidence.

CANCER DESCENDANT

You seek relationships where you're made to feel like one of the family, where your every need and demand is met, particularly emotionally. You want to feel warm and fuzzy and protected by those you love.

LEO DESCENDANT

You're drawn to someone who is strong, confident and outgoing with a busy social life but who can also give you warmth and passion when required. You're attracted to those who can make you laugh and sweep you off your feet.

VIRGO DESCENDANT

You long for kindness and tenderness in a partnership, along with reliability. You want someone who can bring order into your life and who will think things through in a methodical way. Nothing should be left to chance.

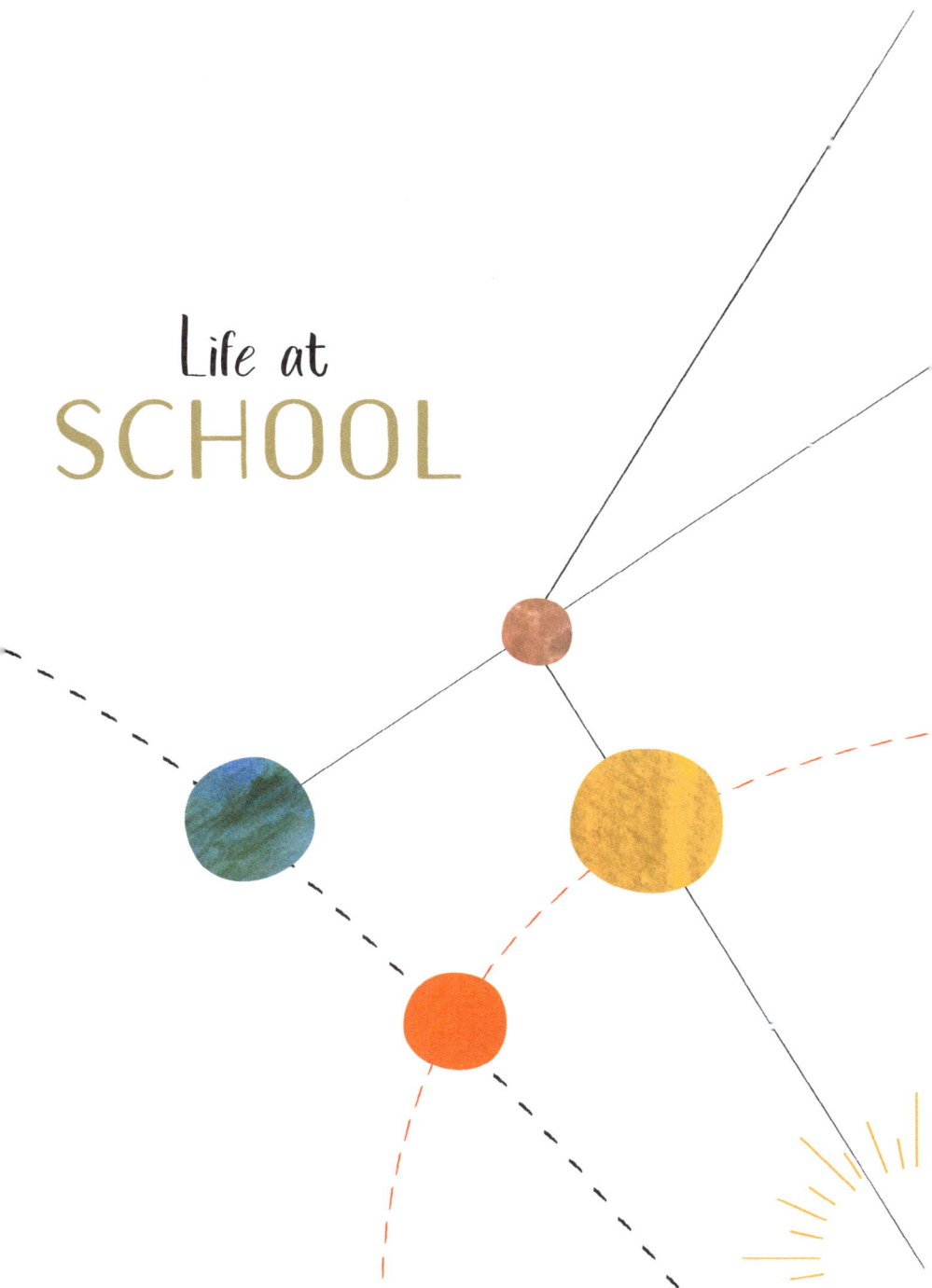

WORKING WONDERS

Have you ever been told that your years at school will be 'the best of your life'? Do you think they will be? Why? Many different things will determine how much you enjoy your school days. And there are sure to be ups and downs along the way. But there are a couple of important factors that astrology can help with. The first is determining your skills and strengths, and the second is learning to work well with others. Identifying your natural interests and abilities can help you to develop a sense of purpose, and it's this that is most likely to motivate you to work hard and actually have fun while you do it. To have a sense of purpose, you need to know yourself and what it is you want from your life. Not what others want for you, or what is expected of you, but what actually makes you come alive.

HIDDEN TALENTS

Not all of your attributes will be immediately obvious. Just because you're a Virgo doesn't mean you are always sensible, for example. You can think about what a typical Virgo might be good at, but you are unique, and the stars are only a guide. Think about your strengths – both emotional and physical. The examples on the right may strike a chord with you, or you might want to create your own list.

BECAUSE YOU'RE ... ANALYTICAL

You use facts and logic when making decisions. Ruled by the head rather than the heart, you are not easily swayed in emotional arguments. You are excellent with data.

Maybe you could be a ...
statistician, scientist, nutritionist, computer engineer

BECAUSE YOU'RE ... DETERMINED

You enjoy completing tasks and persevere to finish what you started. You work hard to reach your goals and keep going even when things aren't working out.

Maybe you could be a ...
welder, estate agent, tax inspector

BECAUSE YOU'RE ... ORGANIZED

You like to plan before taking action. You are well organized and good at sticking to deadlines, using targets and routines to get things done.

Maybe you could be a ...
librarian, urban planner, events manager

BECAUSE YOU'RE ... CAUTIOUS

You are a careful thinker and prefer one-on-one communication to large groups. You don't like to take risks, have good judgment and a talent for solving problems.

Maybe you could be a ...
doctor, accountant, air traffic controller, researcher

BECAUSE YOU'RE ... CONSCIENTIOUS

You are responsible and hard-working, purposeful and determined. You tend to plan in advance and focus on finishing tasks that you've started. You feel bad when you don't manage to complete something.

Maybe you could be a ...
housekeeper, personal assistant

FAMOUS VIRGO PEOPLE

Beyoncé Knowles – *Singer and songwriter*
Blake Lively – *Actor*
Mary Shelley – *Author*
Prince Harry – *British Prince*
Hugh Grant – *Actor*
Stephen Fry – *Author and actor*
Mother Teresa – *Missionary*

TEAM WORK

Working together with others is essential for almost any career path you choose to follow in later life. School can be competitive, yet working in collaboration with your peers rather than against them builds skills that today's employers are looking for.

Here's how well you work together with . . .

ARIES

With your attention to detail and practical skills, you're a valuable member of any team, and especially for a sometimes impatient Aries. You both have excellent organizational skills, so will work brilliantly together on big projects, and while you're happy for Aries to take the lead, you're no pushover.

TAURUS

You two risk getting bogged down with the detail, which can have its advantages but might slow you down at times. It's not that you don't work hard – you both have great work ethics – but someone needs to keep driving things forwards. Set your goals early on and stick to the schedule.

GEMINI

There's bound to be lots of great ideas when you two get your intellectual heads together, although you don't necessarily have the same approach to work. You have a sharper eye for detail, so use it to your advantage and make sure your work is polished and consistent. It will pay off in the long run.

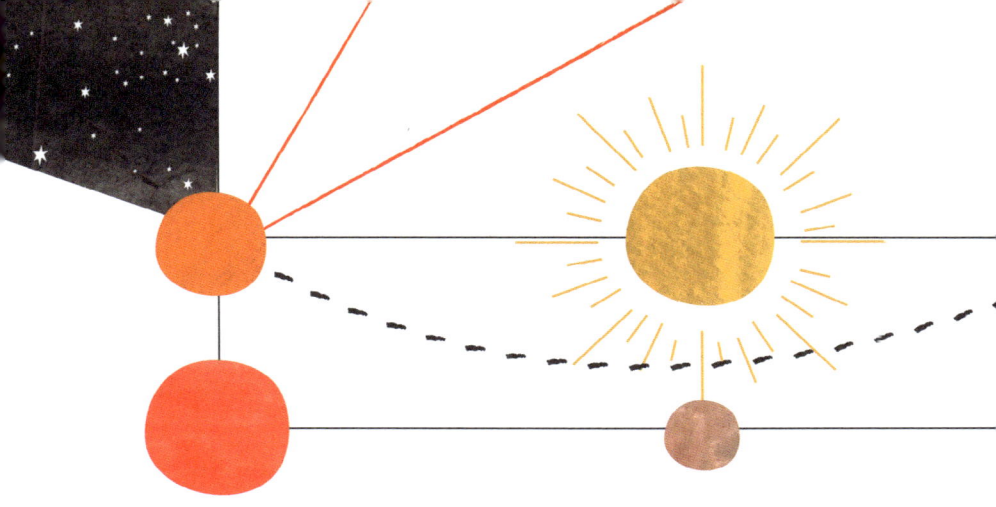

CANCER

Two avid minds are better than one, so this is a winning collaboration. Just be careful not to get obsessed with the smaller details. There's nothing wrong with aiming for perfection, but know when to call it a night and take a step back every now and again to look at the bigger picture.

LEO

If managed well, this unlikely pairing can be successful. It's all about appreciating each other's strong points and applying them appropriately. Simply put, Leo needs to be prepared to apply the brakes to give you time to perfect things, and you need to let imperfections go in order not to cramp Leo's style.

VIRGO

There won't be anything left to chance when two Virgos work together. You will have worked meticulously and methodically, ensuring perfection at every stage. The only trouble is, you might be so hung up on the details you've missed the deadline. Make sure one of you keeps an eye on the clock.

LIBRA

You might be Zodiac neighbours, but working as a team doesn't always come naturally to you two. While Virgo will be head down, getting on with it, Libra is busy trying to work for the common good. To avoid resentment, remember that ultimately you both want the same thing – to do the best you can.

SCORPIO

As long as you give it time to develop, wonderful things can come out of a Scorpio–Virgo partnership. Scorpio might need to tread carefully at first, but they will eventually earn your trust and bring out the best in you. Embrace each other's differences and you could be a powerful pair.

SAGITTARIUS

It's not always easy sailing when you two come together, but it's not for lack of trying. Your perfectionism works best when it's focused on the minute details, while Sagittarius's time is better spent taking in the bigger picture and painting with a broader brush.

CAPRICORN

You two are a great team. Neither of you are afraid of a bit of hard work and don't mind putting in some long hours, at the risk of being workaholics. You like to follow procedures and are disapproving of those who don't. Others might tell you to lighten up, but you're happy the way you are.

AQUARIUS

You both have a lot to bring to the table but don't always give each other credit. Try to remember that Aquarius is bravely pushing boundaries, and explain to Aquarius that you just want to do things properly. Start appreciating each other's attributes, and you could be a force to be reckoned with.

PISCES

Provided you both have clearly defined roles, you can be a highly effective team. Your organizational skills combined with Pisces' natural intuitiveness mean the sky is the limit, particularly when it comes to customer-facing tasks. Just be careful not to tread on each other's toes.

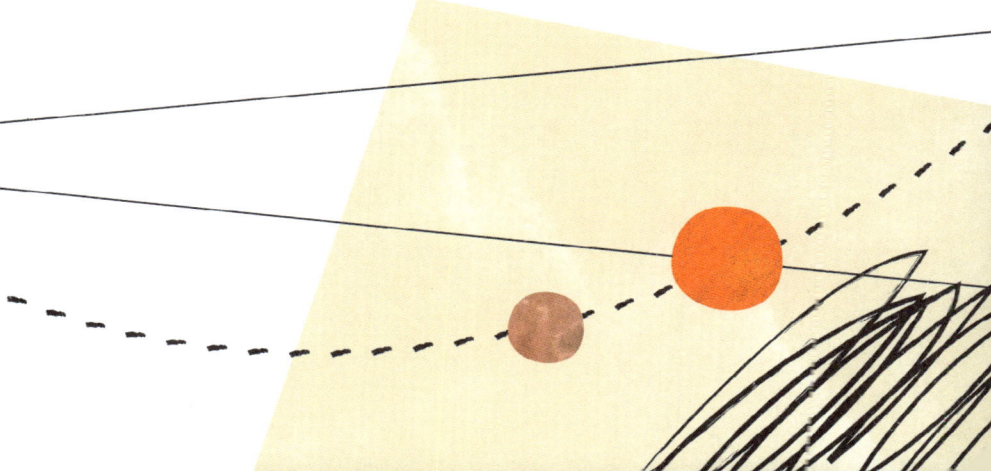

First published 2019
by Ammonite Press
an imprint of Guild of Master Craftsman Publications Ltd
Castle Place, 166 High Street, Lewes, East Sussex, BN7 1XU
United Kingdom

www.ammonitepress.com

Copyright in the Work © GMC Publications Ltd, 2019

Editorial: Susie Duff, Jane Roe, Rachel Roberts, Paul Wade
Designer: Jo Chapman
Illustrations: Sara Thielker
Cover illustration: Sara Thielker

ISBN 978-1-78145-399-5

All rights reserved

No part of this publication may be reproduced, stored in a retrieval system
or transmitted in any form or by any means (including electronic, mechanical, photocopying,
recording or otherwise) without prior written permission from the publisher

The publishers can accept no legal responsibility for any consequences arising from the
application of information, advice or instructions given in this publication

A catalogue record for this book is available from the British Library

Colour reproduction by GMC Reprographics
Printed and bound in China

AMMONITE
PRESS